broken little pieces
Invisible

By Kizmat L. Tention

www.brokenlittlepieces.com

ISBN 9781549755255

Contents

His hand was always there. To
the world you were invisible,
but He always saw you. He
was always there. You were
never alone.
-Message to my invisible
soul

Prologue

How ironic that he had to die in order for me to live.

Broken Little Pieces began as a tribute to my son, Justus. But as I began to write, I realized Broken Little Pieces encompassed more than Justus. It's too vast to narrow down to one life-changing event. My story is too vast to share only that one piece of my life when there are other pieces just as sharp, painful, and impactful as losing my son.

The pain of birthing a stillborn baby is one of the hardest to endure. I needed to pay homage to Justus, to aid in my healing. In the process, I began to heal in other aspects of my life, and this book went in a completely different direction. I was able to become reacquainted with myself. Writing this book has altered my life forever.

In essence, writing helped me realize I was broken in more than one area. I was broken as a woman, mom, and wife. The death of Justus put me on the path to discovering the root of my brokenness. How ironic that he had to die in order for me to live.

I never expected this book to take me on a journey of assiduous introspection and emotional turmoil. This book was not supposed to unleash this wave of uncontrollable tears and exhaustive emotions that had been bottled up for so long. I felt attacked, blindsided, and betrayed. I worked so hard and so long to appear whole and completely put together. It was as if someone opened Pandora's box and all control was completely lost. I felt dark and empty, not knowing which way would truly lead me to the light. Where do you go when you can't see anything but black?

This book that was intended for you, Reader, was now being exposed for what it truly was: healing for me. I was set up by myself. If I had originally thought this book was for me, it probably never would have been written. I convinced myself that everything I had gone through in life was to help someone else, even losing my baby. That's what we're told, right? We go through pain and difficulty to help others. My tag line was that I lost my baby in order to help someone else get through it, but that was bull.

I said this book was for you, but I'm not sure I really meant it or believed it. I always said that she, whoever she is, was worth it. I thought that my losing my baby was worth it for her, but I never stopped to contemplate the notion of that woman I helped being me. What if I went through all of those things to help myself?

I don't think I would've ever convinced myself that I was worth it. I was unable to fathom the thought of being worth the pain and heartache. You, Reader, were my cover-up. You were the way I was able to so eloquently explain things away. You, the woman I have never met, the woman who would one day lose her baby too, would be the one whom I would sweep in to rescue on my big white horse -. I thought I would rescue you from the pain of losing your baby, the pain of losing yourself in marriage or your kids. I would be your hero. However the storyline switched from being about losing him to finding me.

I thought I would be like your God, your saviour. I would bring deliverance and healing, convincing myself that it was in His name of course. I was the messenger of God, chosen for this mission for all the hurting moms like myself. So, yeah, the same tagline I used to convince myself that I was on a mission was the very thing used to compel me to begin this book: the belief that I was helping YOU.

Now I can only sit back and laugh at myself with 20/20 hindsight. The truth is that I just wasn't that into you. It has, and I have, always been so selfishly about me. I don't think it was ever intentional but rather a means for survival. People either take the high road or the low road to overcome hurt and pain. I took the low road. I took what I felt was the more humbling route. I chose the path that seemed to be of the least amount of bitterness and hate. In my mind, making it all about you is what would be deemed more appropriate. Throwing on a cloak of false righteousness and humility made the situation appear to be a win-win for me. I could simultaneously help and heal.

It wasn't until I got deeper into Broken Little Pieces, that I realized my choice was merely a way to deflect and avoid my true pain. It was a well-played and calculated defense mechanism. It was an attempt to hide and avoid my brokenness. I was broken in so many little pieces that I couldn't see where the pieces would begin or end. Trying to help you was the glue holding it all together. The more I focused on you, the less I would focus on me. I mastered being so connected to you, yet I was so disconnected from myself.

Helping others is not a bad thing, but it certainly led to unhealthy outcomes for me. However, despite my disillusioned reasoning at times, I genuinely want you to heal. Parading around appearing to have it all together, but being broken and exhausted inside from pretending to be present, happy, and strong isn't an alien concept to me. I'm well acquainted with feeling unappreciated and invisible. I know what it's like to give my all to ensure the happiness of others. I understand being alone but surrounded by many as life barrels full speed ahead while you remain motionless, watching. It's as if happiness is only meant for others.

Sharing my story is intended to help you realize how living an invisible life causes a girl to grow up and become an invisible wife. You will understand how what seems to be a miniscule part of childhood can define, shape and impact your life. Invisible girls grow up to be invisible wives. Those invisible wives eventually raise invisible children, thereby perpetuating the cycle. The Invisible Wife brings light to your cycle. It puts the spotlight on the masks you have placed on your invisible face. In the end, this light brightens your path for your journey to find the woman you lost, or never knew, once you are willing to remove the masks and allow yourself to be seen.

It's my hope, for your life and marriage never to be the same. Please be warned: The process will not be pretty. However, you owe it to yourself, your true self, to begin the journey. This journey is for every woman who feels as if she can't breathe, for every woman sitting on the sideline, watching life pass her by. It's for every woman screaming with no sound, for every invisible woman. And for me.

Although you feel invisible, I see you. I recognize the signs and the behaviors because I've exhibited them my entire life. I can't say I have it all together now because I'm still trying to repair some of my broken little pieces. My heart's desire is for you to learn to stop and breathe again. It's that first deep breath that lets you know you're alive, that lets you know it's not too late for you. Breathe. Know you're not alone, and I'm right here with you. I feel you. I see you. Broken Little Pieces may be how our story begins, but it certainly doesn't determine how our story ends.

ONE

"Consequences"

...a woman in her forties can be haunted by who she was in her twenties

JUDGE ME BECAUSE I used sex for power, dated for money, and married for money. I figured if I was going to write a book, I should begin with the most shameful, the dirtiest, and the darkest experiences. I saw no need to share this book, in the same manner I've shared my life, invisibly with a mask. I know that is not easy to comprehend. How can I be invisible with a mask? Keep reading.

It baffles my mind that a woman in her forties can be haunted by who she was in her twenties. It sounds absurd, but this is what happened to me. I grew up, had kids and then caused them to think struggle, temptation, and mistakes were incapable of touching them or me. I forgot I had been an adolescent girl who got away with a multitude of things.

For example, during high school, I once called the school, impersonating my mother, and informing them that I was home sick. My poor imitation caused them to contact my mother at work, prompting her to come home in a rage to check on me. She would have caught my boyfriend and me having sex if I hadn't quickly hidden him in the closet and then curled up on the couch, pretending to be sick. Despite her suspicious search of the house, she didn't find him and returned to work, leaving me with the words, "You better not be lying to me, Kizmat Lester!"

It wasn't the words my mother spoke but the look of anger and rage on her face that are so vivid in my memory. Maybe she felt, if she showed her anger, she could protect me from her same path: having a child out of wedlock. My mother had my oldest sister before she met and married my father. -In that case, I wish she would've sat down and talked to me about the path I was on. I wish she'd explained her mistakes and regrets. I wish she'd shared her life experience with me, using compassion and love. I needed her to read beyond the surface, - to look deeper and give words to what I couldn't identify within myself. I needed her to know I just wanted to be seen, that in that moment, sex with my boyfriend was the only way I knew to achieve that. I wish we could've spoken about birth control, protection, or even abstinence. I wish she had told me she loved me and God did too, and that they both wanted better for my life.

Nothing was said, and the incident involving my boyfriend was never brought up again. She walked out the door and went back to work as if nothing ever happened. It could have been—and should have been—a positive, defining moment in my life. It could have been a turning point for me in a positive direction, but her silence gave me a sense of false courage. I'd gotten away with having sex with a boy under my parents' roof. If I did it once, I could do it again.

I never had anyone back in the house, but the lying and thrill of the entire event was exciting to me. Lying became my new norm. What my children get in trouble for can't begin to compare with what I did, without getting caught. Getting caught was just an illusion in my mind because there was no expedient consequence. The very actions I believed I'd gotten away with, unscathed, are the choices that have haunted me.

Now, in my forties, I realize getting caught allows the consequences to be dealt with right away, and skating by is a curse. You do something, get caught, deal with the consequences and move on. My stories don't have that ending so I found myself haunted by my past. I was caught and cursed in my mind. Did my parents know all the secrets I kept? Will my children lie, sleep around, steal, and do a host of other crazy things I did. When will I reap what I have sown from my children? That fear is scarier than the fear I had when my mom stormed into the house on that day. What will I do? What will I say to them? Will I see them? Will they hear me? Will I receive a healthy dose of karma if a woman chooses to ignore my husband's ring as I ignored a ring?

I remember the first time I kissed a married man. Subconsciously, I knew it was wrong, but I was drawn to the thrill and excitement of him. I remember he looked at me with lustful desire. He looked at me as if he could see me. It was a look that I had never seen before. His eyes had so much want and desire in them for me. For the first time, I felt like a man could truly see me.

However, the effect I had on him empowered me; it was like an intoxicating drug. The power was my high and the sensation was addictive. I had stepped into a deeper realm which carried much higher consequences, but I had to play it all the way out. I wanted to see how far to the edge I could go.

My confidence was rooted in my feelings of invincibility. He stroked my ego in the worst way. He gave me sexual power in a way I never expected. I wanted to have the same sexual effect on my husband. I wanted him to tell me how addicting my body was to him. I needed to know he craved to take a hit of me, like a drug. All this that I needed and wanted from him was necessary to feed my addiction of sexual affirmation, desire, and visibility.

It never happened. He never told me the things previous lovers told me. He wasn't addicted. It seemed the more I gave it to him, the less he desired it. And the more insecure I became. The more I needed him to affirm and validate me, the less he did. I felt invisible. Was this invisibility my payback, my true-life karma playing out daily in the intimate moments of my marriage?

The desires I hid and stories I wanted to erase are not pretty. Those stories are the ugly parts of me. The ugly and shameful parts always felt like the most defining. How did I get here? How did I go from a quiet kid to a teen sleeping around with a married man?

TWO

"Invisible Middle Child"

I became known as the prodigal child. I never really knew what that meant, but I accepted it as the invisible child.

RECENTLY, WHILE OUT SHOPPING with my mother, we ran into someone she knew. My mother introduced me, and the individual was shocked to find there was another daughter, a middle daughter. My mother responded with such ease, "Oh, this is the one no one knows." This solidified my mother's knowledge of my invisibility. I can say, I was slightly intrigued standing there and hearing the words flow from my mother's mouth. I knew then, with unwavering certainty, my mother knew all this time: I was the invisible child. I still am.

I wondered why my mother didn't try to help me feel more visible while she was raising me. I

19

was the middle child of three girls. I'd never heard of the phrase "Middle Child Syndrome" until later in my adult life. Apparently I had been self-diagnosed for years without ever knowing it. I always felt different, but never really knew how to articulate nor translate my feelings as a child. According to most research, middle child syndrome is defined as the middle child feeling neglected or left out. I like to define it as the middle child feeling invisible.

I realized, while writing Broken Little Pieces, I've felt invisible my entire life. I went unseen from childhood to adulthood. I was invisible to people I saw on a regular basis throughout my formative years and beyond. I couldn't articulate what that feeling was then, but I knew it was there. Invisibility became a second skin, and seamlessly transitioned with me from year to year. When you're invisible, you can easily adapt to your environment, like a chameleon, easily blending in.

I learned to blend into the background of my family. I did it so effortlessly, many didn't know my parents had a middle daughter. But to the few who knew, the three of us were collectively known as "the Lester girls". There was nothing standout about me as a kid. I didn't have any special gifts or talents that would cause one to notice me. Even my parents spoke of us as a single unit, "the girls." We seldom were addressed as individuals. My mom would say, "Let's go, girls." "Get in the car, girls." "Girls, get ready for church." "Girls, go to bed." We were even punished as one. I remember my older sister and I set a doll on fire and hid it under the bed. I can't recall who the instigator -of the master plan was, but it didn't matter. We were both equally punished.

The bottom line is, from my perspective, I wasn't raised as an individual, but as a member of a group. My childhood resembled a girl group; one or two members shined brightly, while the other - was there for decoration and a few notes in the background. My sisters shined bright enough to be noticed, and then there was me.

I was in the shadows of the stage, unnoticed by the crowd or the management team, who were my parents. I didn't realize the lifelong effect this would have on me. If I'd known then what I know now, I would've screamed for help. I would've begged them to understand the long-term effects of having an invisible child. I would've warned them by giving them a glimpse of how this would shape me in my teens, twenties, thirties, and forties. I would make my parents privy to the significance of raising me as a unit and not as an individual. I would cry out over and over until I was heard. There's no way I would remain silent in letting them know. Being the invisible child was the beginning of a life of wearing masks that would take me a lifetime to remove. Being unseen shaped me as a parent and wife.

When I think about how I was as a child, it all makes perfect sense. I was more attached to adults outside of the home (i.e. my great grandmother). I never went to my parents for advice or help, and I was definitely more independent than my sisters. I never really felt like I belonged, and I often wondered if I was secretly adopted, with other parents out there somewhere.

I never got along with my siblings, and I felt my parents favored them over me. I felt no connection to my mom, dad, or anyone else living in my household. I was the outcast, the black sheep. I was the misfit, the outsider, the invisible child.

Well, I sought to be seen in places outside of my home and church. I believe the allure of drugs, gangs and the inability to leave bad relationships stems from children, adolescents, and adults going out searching for a place to emotionally connect and belong-— a place to be seen and to feel as though - they matter. I didn't join a gang or do drugs, but I did turn to the streets, in my adolescent years, and to the life - they offered.

I quickly learned that - my idea of love was directly connected to money, fancy cars, and street respect. The street always accepted me and made me feel warm and accepted. In my young mind, anything that happened in the streets took priority over church events and services. I ran to the place where I felt I didn't have to pretend, to fake it, or to act. I could be myself, whoever that was. I had all the same issues outside of the church as I did inside, but somehow the street life felt more authentic.

However, I soon realized that as authentic as I thought the street life was to me, I wasn't authentic to it. I found I was pretending. I pretended the streets and riotous living brought happiness. - I was empty and so were the people with whom I associated. Many are still empty, searching for a connection by clinging to relationships, friendships, careers, and religions, to no avail.

I jokingly became known as the prodigal child in my home. I never really knew what that meant, but I accepted and interpreted it as the invisible child. The child who was unknown and lacked any talent or gifts deemed important in the church. The word "prodigal," in my head, was no different - from the term bastard or black sheep.

With my father being a Youth Pastor and my mother a First Lady, it was not acceptable to be uninvolved in church. Being invisible at church automatically meant being invisible at home. As a result, the words prodigal or black sheep were only able to slam against that protective casing and shatter. Only my great grandma, Nancy, could see the girl inside the shell. She always wrapped me in hugs, showered me with love, and made me feel special. In her arms I had peace.

I wonder how having an invisible child made my parents feel. If I were them, I would've been saddened if people didn't realize I had another child, especially the middle child. As an adult, I wish they would have noticed or done something differently. I don't know exactly what I wish they would've done, but I wonder if I would've had fewer negative experiences and felt less empty had my parents shown some emotion about having an invisible child. Had they shown they cared, it's possible, I wouldn't have had a magnified craving for attention as an adult. I grew up to become the little unknown girl all over again, fighting to be noticed, to be liked, to feel loved, and to be seen. If they would have shown emotion, I would have known it was acceptable for me to do the same. I would have tried to express emotion about feeling invisible more effectively.

In retrospect, I was crying out for help through my actions. I cried out when I began to kiss boys in my neighborhood, or when I began to hide and watch porn or look at Playboy. I was crying out, but no one heard me. No one heard me attempting to let them know that I was still a person, with or without church. I was desperately crying for my parents to see me regardless of their titles. I needed them to acknowledge me even though I couldn't sing the house down, or usher, or do anything else at church. I wanted them to separate church from home. I needed Mom and Dad, not Pastor and First Lady. I needed them to realize home was their first ministry.

I felt like I was in a dream, trapped and muffled. I screamed, but there was no sound. I stood there screaming with all my might, with my eyes squeezed tightly together, and my fists clenched; yet nothing but dry air escaped from my lungs. I tried to run, but my feet were heavy lead blocks, firmly settled on the ground. Help me!! Can anyone hear me?! Can anyone see me?! My heart was racing, and my breathing became more shallow as I continued to release dry air and simultaneously attempted to lift my lead feet. I wanted to wake up!! Relief finally came when I came back to consciousness and could be seen and heard. I am awake now, and it only took over thirty years.

THREE

"Finding Visibility"

Growing up a Pastor's Kid, P.K., blurred the lines of church life and home life. In fact, there was no line as far as I was concerned. Church was home, and home was church. It seemed like we were in church around the clock. It was like the thorn in my side. There was never anything new or exciting about church, it was just a ritual, being around the same people, doing the same thing: Dress up, show up, hear a sermon, talk to people, and go home.

I was raised in a church where everything was about your title or your name. Everyone catered to the bishop, pastors, missionaries, deacons, and mothers. I couldn't care less what title people wore. I connected with those who were sweet, kind, and a joy to be around. Church was not a place of worship for me. It was more like school, somewhere you had to go because you really didn't have a choice. I never felt like anything I did was ever supported or encouraged because it usually had nothing to do with the church. I tolerated church, the people, and counted down the days of church like I counted down the days to my graduation.

I didn't hate the church; I just despised people who did not live authentic lives. This caused me to be very judgmental of people, especially my sisters. I was quick to call them out for being fake Christians. I never claimed to be a Christian, but I was always quick to point out those I felt were living double lives.

I felt this way about my older sister and all of her church friends. I felt they were no different from me; they just used the church as a cover-up. My oldest sister loved church, and I never understood why. I could think of a million other places I would rather be. I had acquaintances in the church but never any true friends, and there was rarely much contact with them outside of church.

Church felt like a place of rules that only consisted of the things you could not do. Don't drink, don't smoke, don't wear

pants, don't lie, don't steal —and
every other don't you could possibly
think of. They made me feel like
God was this higher being whose
purpose was only to make sure we
didn't break any rules. I felt like
people "played church", and I never
saw anything in them that gave me
a desire to serve God. I never heard
a message preached that made me
want to be a better person or give up
my so-called sinful lifestyle. Only
fear was preached and rarely the
grace and love of God. My
relationship, or lack thereof, with
God was all about obligation. Go to
church and, hopefully, you won't
end up in hell. The more hours
spent in the church, the fewer hours
spent in the club.

I never understood why my
church denomination seemed to
have so many rules in comparison
to others. For example, the women
couldn't wear pants. They only
wore skirts and dresses down to
their ankles. All I could ever think
was, whose bright idea was this? It
had to be some super religious and
overly spiritual man. I can't tell you
how many times I almost busted my

head wide open tripping over my skirt. Luckily, my parents never enforced that ridiculous rule outside of church. But, surely, wearing long skirts wasn't a guaranteed ticket into heaven. Lord knows I saw my share of girls who wore long skirts leaving the house, but had jeans tucked in their bags to change into once they were out.

Growing up, this form of religion was referred to as "sanctified," and I was determined never to identify with them or the title. In my opinion, church was no different - from the county jail where you were given a uniform and a list of rules to obey to avoid punishment. I didn't fit in, and I never really tried to. I just went because I lived in my parent's house, and we weren't given an option. I feared God too much to pretend I was ready to give my life to Him.

I don't know at what point I began to notice people didn't know me or notice me. I was the quiet one and didn't realize it. I don't remember being shy; I just didn't have much to say. I remember times when I'd be with my parents, and someone would ask who I was. After my parents responded, people were always surprised I was the middle daughter. Everybody knew my older sister because she could sing and was really involved in church. Everyone knew my younger sister as well because she was the baby girl, and the baby is always loved. Plus, she was a loveable child. Perhaps she also was known because she looked so much like my father, the Youth Pastor, and people find ways to attach themselves to authority.

  I don't think I purposely hid or avoided attention in the church. I think I was just comfortable doing my own thing, and I was never one for making sure that everyone knew me. I would go to church, sit in the back, and usually just go to sleep. I'm still the same way when I'm around my family in a church environment; I stay back and to myself, being okay with being the outsider, the anomaly.

  Having a title or being gifted in some way were key to being known and visible. My lack of interest and true involvement in church made me invisible there, even though I religiously attended. As I grew into my tween and adolescent years, my focus began to shift, and my involvement in the church went from very little — children's choir and ushering — to non-existent. I was the worst singer ever, and once you get beyond the kids choir, in my church, you really had to know how to sing.

So I tried being an usher. Although the head usher was very mean, I liked him. I loved how he gave direction with authority and force, never really seeming to care who was offended. He had a job to do, and he did it well. But ushering didn't last.

Once, on Youth Sunday, I had to take a note to my father, who was sitting in the pulpit of the church. As I was walking up the stairs to the pulpit, during service, I literally tripped up the stairs. We all have that moment of tripping up stairs, = when a graceful recovery evades us. Well, gracefulness sprinted away from me in front of an entire church. I handed the note to my father, walked back down the stairs, and out the side door. That was the beginning and the end of my ushering career. At that point, my parents realized there was no longer a need to force my involvement in church activities.

My older sister thrived and loved being heavily involved in church activities, but my interest began to turn towards boys. I was no longer the shy and quiet little girl. I'd noticed I was becoming quite cute, and the boys took notice, too. They were beginning to show me attention and, I began to love it. I was the cute, flat-chested girl with a gap in her teeth. I was a fast runner, and that went over well with the boys in my neighborhood.

The more I was noticed outside of the church, the less it mattered to me what happened in the church. Early on, I began to pay attention to who was noticed. I don't remember all of my childhood crushes, but I do remember the boys that weren't interested. Outside of church, the rules felt very different. The expectations of being a girlfriend were much higher. Kissing and touching were the norm in the neighborhood in my elementary school years. This was probably the beginning of my growing ego when it came to boys.

I found myself caring even less that adults didn't notice I was cute or that they didn't even know me. I was more interested in knowing their sons thought I was cute and knew I existed. I wouldn't date the boys in the church, but I loved that they were interested in me. The cat-and-mouse chase was beginning, and it became my sole interest in church. I would bait and catch them only to turn around to leave them in limbo until the next convention or large church gathering.

I had no interest in the boys at my local church. Maybe this was because they seemed boring to me, and I had known most of them all of my life. Instead, I rebelled by seeking the attention of boys at church conventions and other events where boys outside my local church were sure to be. -

I think part of my rebelliousness was payback towards my parents — payback for being forced to go to church constantly and attend all of those Godless conventions, which felt as if they were more about money and less about God. If I didn't feel like the purpose of those conventions was to connect with God, then why should I attend?

Finally, I found a purpose in the church that made sense to me: Pursue the cute boys. The goal was to have them wrapped around my finger, or so I thought. Along with my growing interest in boys, I became focused on school sports. I remember someone always arriving to pick me up after my games, but the stands were void of family cheering me on during the games. I was a cheerleader in middle school, played basketball, and ran track three years in high school. I was accomplished in sports and have great memories, but the most - salient or noticeable or striking memory in my mind is the painful absence of my parents. Every year and for every sport, my parents were absent because they were at church. I always felt as if church were more important to my parents than supporting me. There was always a church service, function, or event that usurped their time.

Deep down, I was bitter and hurt. I never understood why my parents went to church so much. It felt like there was something going on seven days a week. I thought if heaven was based on church attendance, then surely they would make it in! I believed that I should have come before church at some point. I wasn't trying to replace God in their lives, but I felt like I needed their time, too.

Maybe my parents were only doing what they were taught to do. Maybe they were taking their cues from all of the older parents in the church, or perhaps they were modeling what they thought it meant to have a relationship with God, never realizing that it was the very thing that turned me away from God. Nevertheless, if this is what having a relationship with God looked like, I didn't want it. I didn't want my kids to feel like their interests and activities didn't matter. I didn't want them to experience the lack of support I felt. I loved God. I just wasn't willing to sacrifice my everything to prove it.

I desired my parents' support, encouragement, affirmation and affection towards my sports accomplishments, but I never expressed my need. I tried to pretend it didn't matter. So I made a vow to myself that if I ever had kids, I would never miss one of their events. I would never have them waiting for hours after a practice to be picked up like I had to wait. They would always have a number one fan they could depend on, and it would always be me. To this day, I don't think I've ever missed any of my son's games. I am always the first parent in line to pick up my kids from any practice, rehearsal, or event. That is one vow I made and kept. They will always feel and hear my support and love for them.

Affection and verbal expressions of love were not

modeled for me to learn. I knew we were loved, but there were no hugs or loving words. My home today is a very peaceful place to reside, but I have learned that there is a vast difference between a quiet home and peaceful home. So, I will say I grew up in a quiet home. I never heard my parents argue, fuss, or fight. I just saw them living life. They would get up, go to work, come home, get ready for church, and then repeat. It was very stable and routine. I had family members who'd have shouting matches and fist fights with their parents, but that never happened in our home.

My parents were polar opposites; I never saw them flirt, hug, kiss, or display any type of outward affection toward each other. I didn't think it was odd at the time, but now I wonder why they never seemed to be in love. I can't remember a single time when I saw them hold hands or even kiss. This was my first introduction and example of a relationship, but it wasn't much to go on. I wonder if my mom felt invisible too. I wonder if she craved more in life and more in her marriage. I wonder if she had been an invisible child as well.

Does an invisible child grow up to be an invisible wife? I always felt like my oldest sister was my mom's favorite and my youngest sister was my dad's favorite. Then there was me. I don't recall my sisters getting affection either; it's not like I was purposely left out or treated differently. It was a feeling I had in my mind. I knew I was different. I knew there was something different about me, and neither of my parents could identify with me. I don't know if my sisters or parents felt it or even thought about it. It was how I felt, and I accepted that feeling as my norm. I accepted myself as the outcast in my home, as I did in church.

The two worlds merged. We spent more time at church than with family. We seldom had family vacations, but church-based trips were innumerable. My first trip to Disney World, for example, was with the church. My first trip to the beach was with the church. Any picnics or outings were all usually church outings. Church was our immediate family. We weren't close to my paternal grandmother because she lived in another state. We weren't close to my maternal grandmother either because she didn't raise my mom, or we just weren't around her much. I was closest to my great grandmother, but she also attended our church. Her giving me Wrigley's gum at church is my fondest memory of church. In essence, church was really all I knew, and I understood it to be reflective of a family. I didn't have any true models of what I expected from my family because everyone around me was doing the exact same thing.

So what happens to a child when she feels invisible at the two places that seem to matter the most?

FOUR

"Love Doesn't Live Here"

SINCE I DIDN'T HAVE many examples of fulfilling and loving relationships, I looked elsewhere. I searched for examples that appeared more exciting and fun than my parents. I sought out relationships with a touch of drama and emotion. I had cousins who were able to show me the way to - drama.

They unintentionally taught me love was based on money, the car you drove, and the respect you earned on the street. Somewhere along the way, I had become a self-proclaimed gold digger, and I was in high pursuit of the fast life. This pursuit didn't begin overnight. It began after I carefully observed cousins who dated drug dealers. I became infatuated with the glamorous life. I know now it was only an illusion, because my cousins didn't obtain anything of significant value. Nevertheless, the new hairdos, new outfits, and pocket cash resonated with me.

Honestly, the material perks that came with being a drug dealer's girlfriend I easily could've gotten myself. I think the real value, for me, was the status of the men. I was reckless in my late teens and early twenties. I, like most during that age, thought I was invincible. My insecurity played out as selfish and egotistical. I was cocky and falsely overconfident. In order to keep thoughts of inferiority at bay, I would often come across as heartless with men. I made it my mission to make men feel replaceable and easily discarded. It was, and had to be, all about me and what they could do for me.

Living the fast life seemed fun and adventurous. I enjoyed the thrill until the day I witnessed my boyfriend put a gun to someone's head. I knew it wasn't a game, and I remember feeling the intensity of the situation. The two men were close friends, so I could only assume that they were arguing over something having to do with money or drugs.

I was in the house when his friend pulled into the driveway. My ex went outside, and I heard the heated verbal altercation between them. The sequence of events was occurring so rapidly, I didn't see my ex grab a gun before he went outside. I was shocked when I walked out and saw him firmly press that gun to his friend's head. I remember thinking I was about to be the sole eyewitness to a murder. I screamed for him to stop and come back in the house. Whatever was the root of this dispute, it wasn't worth the cost of lives. It wasn't worth theirs and certainly not mine. This was too real, and I wasn't ready to witness a murder or suffer any of the subsequent consequences.

I'd been living in the fast lane long enough to know retaliation was almost a certainty. Was I willing to die, if I became a target by association, for a person who probably wouldn't shed a tear? I also had a son by that time; what if he were caught in the crossfire? He was only three, and I'd put him in more situations than I'd be willing to admit, because of my immaturity and love for the fast life. Being a witness to all that transpired this day made me realize there was more to my life. I was determined my story wouldn't end here with jail or death.

I refused to continue to be a part of this path. I had no desire to spend my weekends talking to my man with a glass between us and holding life down until his release. I didn't know who I really was at the time, but I knew I wasn't this girl. I had to continue my quest for love elsewhere. Love didn't live in these streets. Seeing a man almost take a life, and the other almost losing his, was a defining moment. Of course, I didn't realize this then, but I certainly realize it now. We all have those life changing moments when you know God's hand and grace were all over you. It's up to you to accept His grace in those moments. Fortunately, I did that day.

FIVE

"You Shole' is UGLY"

I was disappointed with the time and effort wasted "doing" and not enough time just "being"

MY UGLY WAS the piece of me that hurt, and I yearned for love, forgiveness, acceptance, and truth. I can't address it as apiece; it felt like all of me. My entire life screamed failure. My ugly were my mistakes and dirty little secrets. My ugly was the hope my broken pieces wouldn't cut me so deep that I'd bleed out before help arrived. My ugly were the memories of the vulnerable little girl who had to be strong- but secretly just wanted to hide. My ugly was personal, and I held it close to my heart, where no one could see and judge. Every part of my life felt ugly, especially my marriage. My ugly was a vessel to house my regrets, doubts, fears and insecurities about myself and my marriage.

I met my husband at church, of all places. I met him during a time when my feelings of insecurity and false confidence were at an all-time high. Looking back, I was not in a place to be in a relationship. Our courting was short. We were soon engaged and the wedding planning began. I became so focused on planning a wedding that it never dawned on me what our marriage would resemble once the wedding was over.

We married and six months later I was pregnant. So the planning began all over again for another monumental event: the birth of our daughter. My son from a previous relationship was 12, so the birth of our daughter was the perfect addition to make us look like the happy little family. I jumped into my role as a mom and wife, and he as a provider. There was no spark or life to our marriage, just well played roles. Any sense of joy or excitement was always centered around the kids and never our marriage. I ignored the "Happy Wife, Happy Life" mantra and went with the illusion of "Perfect Wife,

Happy Life . . . or at least Fake it 'Til You Make it!"

I have always tried to make it a point to have salad ready for my husband when he gets home from work, because that's what I thought a perfect wife does. He usually walks in the house and goes straight to the refrigerator. If salad is there, he grabs that first.

Not long ago, I mixed a salad with lots of Greek toppings and placed it in the fridge. Once before, he complained that the toppings made the salad soggy, and he'd prefer keeping them separate. On this particular day, I did as he requested. I made sure the lettuce and the Greek mixture were in separate bowls. The cucumbers I added to the mixture formed a small pool of liquid at the bottom of the bowl. He grabbed the bowl and asked, "What's this?" I immediately accelerated to defensive mode, and sarcastically told him the toppings were separated because I remembered his complaint the last time I made it. He calmly responded, "Why are you getting on the defensive as if I'm not allowed to ask any questions? I wasn't complaining. I merely saw all of the liquid at the bottom of the bowl and wanted to know what it was. I didn't know if you added dressing already or possibly something else. But either way, you can't get on the defensive every time I ask a question."

I snapped back, "Well, I try to always make things perfect and exactly the way you asked, and it's never enough!"

He looked solemnly at me, "Why do you think it's never enough? I've never told you that. I don't even complain. Why is everything always about a competition or winning for you? It's not that serious to me, and it shouldn't be to you. What is the real reason you feel this way? As if you always have to win, or be right?"

Instantly, I realized that was the million-dollar question. Why did I always feel the need to win? The only response I could give was that I get tired of taking the blame for everything. I said, "You always let me do stuff and choose things, and secretly hate me for the decisions. I choose the cars, and you hate the cars. I choose the house, and you hate the house. I choose the furniture, and you complain about the furniture. I find myself always trying to make sure I'm not the root of your frustrations, and it goes all the way back to 2003, our wedding. I've had to live with this since we've been married and I'm tired of it!"

Without raising his voice, he replied, "Well, that has less to do with me and more to do with you. You shouldn't feel that way, and I've never given you a reason to feel like that. So you need to relieve that pressure of being a people pleaser. I've never asked that from you, and it's not attractive at all."

It was such an eye-opening conversation, but it was also hard to ingest. It left me with much to ponder. Had I built these expectations in my head and projected them on myself as if they came from him? Could I have misread the situation or our lives that much? Was I utterly wrong? Where did this people-pleasing woman come from? This was another part of my ugly I had to face, and not only face, but I also had to own it. Fear of failure was ugly to me. I feared giving my all and not receiving reciprocity, but yet, the fear molded me into a people pleaser.

I didn't have much to say after that conversation. It was so hard to process. He'd been so kind and gentle with his words that night. It was as if he knew I needed a little extra care. I wasn't sad; instead, I was disappointed about the time and effort wasted "doing" and not enough time just "being." Being what? Just being me.

I needed validation as a wife, as a mom, and as a woman. It was merely a want, but I made it a need. I thought a wealth of validation was what I needed to justify my marriage and role as a wife. I wanted to be seen, felt, and heard. He did see me all along. As much as I didn't want to be invisible, I was more frightened because he could see me. If he truly saw me, he knew I wasn't the perfect wife I pretended to be. It had been such an internal battle between being seen and unseen in my head. In one aspect, I wanted him to see me, but in another I didn't.

I wanted him to think I measured up to the criteria of a perfect wife, yet I was afraid he might realize that I really was not that perfect at all. I wanted him to come home and not want for anything; yet, I waited in fight-or-flight mode, ready to protect myself from his unspoken expectations that were all in my head. My expectations were so twisted, his only options were to stroke my ego or attack my ego. Why couldn't I just cook, clean, dress, or do anything without using everyday tasks to define me as a wife? I mastered simultaneously screaming "SEE ME! SEE ME!" and "Don't see me. Don't see me in case it doesn't work in my favor. Just do unto me what has always been done. Treat me as if I'm invisible."

I decided it was time to take a hard look at myself, no longer looking solely at my husband. After all, we married each other, and we both have our respective places. People can't be married to themselves. I longed for that undeniable spark I'd see between other couples. I needed to see love manifested in my marriage by the simple things like date nights and holding hands in public. I was ready to put in the work to remove all hindrances, strongholds, and fear, for the salvation of my marriage. If my marriage was going to stand a chance, I had to address every piece of ugly.

I'd wasted time being ashamed of my ugly, and I rarely took the time to process it. Finally, after years, I decided to stare my ugly in the face to save my marriage. I opened the closet door to greet my ugly, and my view was filled with my face! The scarred and ugly person filled with darkness, who I'd carried with me for a lifetime, was staring back at me. I was taking a hard and deep look at myself! I was dark and cold, above all, shocked at my own appearance.

I had been smothered by fear of being exposed and judged by others for so long, but standing there, looking at the ugly version of myself, it dawned on me how petrified I'd really been of being exposed to myself. I'd been pretending so long I'd learned not to look at myself. I'd figured if I never viewed myself, I wouldn't have to face the scars, the phantom weight of self-inflicted judgments. As long as I didn't look inward and say, "You shole is ugly," as a character, said in "The Color Purple," I wouldn't have to change. I wouldn't have to be real with myself or others. I could just continue as I'd been.

But I didn't want to go on pretending, blaming, deflecting, and exhausting myself and those close to me. I sure was ugly — empty eyes full of shame, guilt, and regret. Those same eyes beheld the marred heart that beat in my chest. Others could see through the facade. They could see my ugly. They could see me. Now, I could see me, too.

I wanted to slam the closet door and barricade my ugliness and deformities inside! I didn't want to see, and didn't want anyone else to see this horror. I felt the burdensome breathing of my ugly surrounding me. I wanted to turn my back and run away. I wanted to escape from myself. I wanted to flee what I'd willingly greeted. That would have been easier than dealing with this.

Running, escaping and suppressing had been the methods I had used and it clearly hadn't worked. This time, I would stay here, in a standoff between my past and my future. Ready to fight the life I had, to get to the life I wanted.

It is always easier to stay in a familiar situation, even if it is bad, rather than taking the plunge into the unknown. I'm a life coach. How could I coach someone else if I wasn't willing to address my own ugly issues? I was able to gather myself because I knew I had power, and my life and my marriage were hanging in the balance. I also realized that at this point, I had nothing to lose. I couldn't get any lower or feel more broken and rejected — all self-inflicted, of course. I got to a point where I just knew it was time — time for change — time for authenticity, time for truth.

I was willingly approaching my ugly for a conversation, and this removed my fear of being controlled, manipulated, or exposed. I was no longer afraid to see who I was, or who I had become, due to my past. I began to look at what I deemed as ugly skeletons, and saw beauty in them. My ugly now allowed me to make mistakes and grow. Now my ugly allowed me to be human and removed the notions of perfectionism and pretending. It showed me I'd have to get down and dirty before I could come up clean. By no longer being ashamed, I began to peel back the layers, exposing my authentic self. My ugly had been all encompassing, but one day I realized my ugly had become my beautiful.

As I began to see the beauty in my ugly, I began to love it. My ugly were no longer the piece of my story I hid; it became the piece I revealed. Now it ushers in hope to people like you or like me. It shows, despite what I've gone through, I can come out on top. I found the beauty of God's grace in my ugly. I was a diamond in the rough. A diamond is never found pretty and shiny. It's first found rough, dirty, and pale. The beauty comes with refining, shaping, and buffing.

Most can't recognize a diamond before it's refined, and the same goes for life. Most people can't see your potential, and you probably can't see it either, but that doesn't mean it isn't there. It doesn't mean that you're not a diamond. A diamond is always a diamond, regardless of whether it's first found in the dirt, during the ugly phase, or on a shelf at the finest jewelry store, shining bright after it has been cleaned and its beauty revealed.

Pieces of me are still ugly, but I know now my ugly is my beautiful. The ugliness holds a beauty only God could behold. And in His timing, others, including myself, would come to see the beauty within the ugliness.

You are the same way. You may be dirty, rough, hurt, ashamed, and disfigured, but with a little TLC— actually, a lot of TLC—you will be shaped into a beautiful diamond, unrecognizable from your beginning state. You are not alone. You are not the only person who's had an abortion, been promiscuous, stolen, broken the law, used drugs, or been an invisible wife. Your ugly is beautiful.

I challenge you to face your ugly head on. When you begin to face it, you'll see growth and strength. You'll see how you survived to tell the story. You'll see how your ugly didn't define you, but it helped shape who you are today. You'll see, just as I did, your ugly is actually your beautiful.

I keep repeating that because sometimes you have to hear something over and over again for it to actually stick. I allowed my ugly to dictate and define the dynamic of my marriage. I projected my ugly insecurities and expected my husband to fill me with validation. I expected him to fill a bottomless pit. I put the pressure on him to pour into a hole, which was impossible to fill, and I blamed him for not giving me validation.

I was invisible and broken before I married, and marriage magnified what was already there. It's not your marriage that is causing all of your heartache and pain; it's the unresolved issues that you brought into your marriage. You will not be able to live a true and authentic life until you stop blaming and pointing fingers at someone else. Look yourself in the mirror and say it's not him, it's me!

Don't be afraid to peel back the layers of your life to figure out the root of your pain. My layers took me all the way back to my childhood. I allowed those layers to become my norm. It was all I knew. Even in the sanctity of my marriage, I still struggled with the fear of being exposed as a fraud. Why do you not feel good enough? Why is it so hard to believe that you are enough, even in your current state? We are all a work in progress and it's possible that we will forever be, but that doesn't mean you can't start the work. That doesn't mean you can't begin the journey of discovering who you were created to be. That doesn't mean that you have to die with your dreams. If you are reading, breathing, or crying right now there is still hope. There is still time. You don't have to believe the lies that someone said about you or the lies you said about yourself. I was broken. I was heart. I felt undeserving of so many things in life. But just because I was emotionally there does not mean I have to stay there.

My inner truth was false and insecure, but my outer truth was what I pretended to be: happy and carefree. It's not a race; it's a journey. And I'm learning daily. You can't look ahead at how far you have to go; that would be overwhelming. Instead, you celebrate your small victories of awareness. You make intentional decisions to aid in your journey. Today you'll have a better attitude. Today I won't get defensive if he asks what type of dressing I used for the salad. I'll just tell him and leave it at that. I'm finally learning to take that pressure and extra weight off myself. At the end of the day, it's really not that serious. And having peace in my

home and mind are more important
than worrying about a soggy salad.

SIX

"Addicted"

"My sense of invisibility had absolutely nothing to do with him and everything to do with me."

Passion, desire, AFFECTION, FIRE, and romance were lacking between my parents. I wanted no parts of that life but somehow managed to have a marriage reflective of my parents. I married a man just like my father. He's an amazing provider and does everything to make sure all of our financial needs are met. Basically, I settled for security.

Security is nice, but I secretly craved passion, romance, and desire. I settled for a quiet marriage —although not peaceful—and assumed passion was not that important. I convinced myself love was different in my home. I told myself that my love was real, even though secretly I felt unfulfilled. Surely, real love was not possible the way it was played out in the recesses of my mind. Real-life love wasn't full of laughter, longing, and the feelings of "I can't live without you." The fantasy I'd conjured, in my imagination, wasn't my reality; therefore, I was convinced my expectations were unrealistic.

No woman truly feels like she can't live without her husband. At least that's what I thought. I'd never felt that way, so it couldn't be a real experience for anyone. In fact, I imagined life without him quite often. I couldn't imagine life without my children, but him, I could do without.

I have a beautiful home. I've never been forced to work a job. I've been blessed to stay home with my children. I shop when I want, without any questioning. We travel, eat out, and appear to be living what some have referred to as the American Dream. How ungrateful I must sound to someone on the outside looking in, but all I had meant nothing when I felt invisible.

My home was very quiet. A quiet home just like the one I was raised in. I'd settled and found myself exhibiting the very behaviors I always wanted to avoid. I was a wife now, and I hadn't done anything differently than the example I'd seen in my parents. My husband and I had our daily routine, just as my parents did. Our children didn't see us fight or argue, as my sisters and I never saw growing up. We didn't show outward signs of love, passion or affection. My marriage was dry. It was dry and longing for moisture, which could only be provided by us, but neither of us yielded to the need. We simply remained quiet, going day in and day out with parched hearts.

The important thing was the quiet, which I equated with peace. But there was a stark difference. There was no peace, because we both had unmet needs. We both were dry heaving the discontent of being in a committed marriage, but a non-intimate one. There was silent, quiet suffering, but not tranquility. The correlation between the invisible wife and the invisible child is adaptation; both adapt to surviving. Surviving was intrinsic to me. If I couldn't do anything else, I knew I could survive. I knew I could keep quiet and pretend, if that is what it took to survive. As long as I could survive and suppress, no one would be the wiser.

I assumed I was skilled at suppressing until the day I had a conversation with someone very close to me. During our conversation, she revealed to me her observations of my marriage. She'd noticed our lack of affection and our disconnect. I was shocked that she noticed, but not surprised because that's how I'd felt for years.

This encounter made me wonder who else had noticed the dryness in my marriage; furthermore, if people outside of my home noticed, surely my daughter noticed. I knew this meant I was modeling for her the same behavior that was modeled for me. I was teaching her that it's normal and acceptable to be an invisible wife as long as there was a beautiful home, a car, and quiet life to show for it. I was conveying to her that she should be an empty shell, and that the shell would sustain her.

My concern was that my example would inevitably lead her to settle and accept the quiet home while ignoring and suppressing her needs and desires as a wife. I was inadvertently showing her never to fight to feel loved and cherished. My actions, could possibly, cause her to become like me: a shopaholic who found validation in material things, or more likely, a woman who sought attention from a source other than her husband.

Outside attention made me an addict. Whenever I felt invisible in my home, the dryness of my marriage was magnified, and so was my inability to convey my thirst to my husband. Instead of talking to him, I found myself intentionally leaving the house, craving and looking forward to compliments. I knew the right people to find, the right outfit to wear, just like I did back in the day with those white shorts. I was, metaphorically, pimping myself out for attention.

I found myself dressing for the attention of other men, not my husband. I justified the behavior in my mind because he wouldn't give me compliments no matter how nice I dressed. I was a woman, and I believed I deserved compliments, to be desired, and to be the apple of someone's eye, if for only a short time. That was my attention addiction speaking to me, and I took heed.

I relished and basked in the attention. It lifted me up and gave me false feelings of ecstasy, validation, completion, quenched thirst, and visibility, until those times I'd have too much of it. Someone would go too far. He'd stare a little too long or make an inappropriate comment. In these sobering moments, I'd process what was going on in my life. I'd ponder the state of my marriage, my emotions, and try to figure why I needed attention from someone else in order to feel pretty and desired.

I didn't admit I had a problem, nor did I allow myself to see the patterns of feeling high and feeling sober. When I finally saw the pattern of this attention addiction, I told my husband. I shared with him my natural tendency to seek outside of the home what I felt was lacking. I thought if I communicated to him that things would change between us, but it never got better.

Being invisible shattered me into so many broken little pieces. I was an invisible child - who grew into an invisible wife. I carried all my broken parts into my marriage, and felt the exact same loneliness from childhood. The more I poured into composing Broken Little Pieces, the more I understood. I began to understand I didn't leave my invisibility in my childhood. I only began to cover it with masks, so that something about me could be seen. I was an invisible wife who wore masks, and it was killing my marriage.

I thought it was him. He had to be the reason I wasn't happy. I felt unsatisfied, unfulfilled, ignored, invisible, and it had to be his fault. I placed the blame on him for the overwhelming - invisibility in my life. I would hold him to all of these unspoken expectations, intentionally setting him up to fail so that I could prove my point. I would flirt with other men when he was too busy to respond to me, to justify my feelings of rejection. I would expect him to buy me gifts even though I knew I was impossible to please.

One year he called me and said, "Hey what do you want for Christmas?" I told him that I didn't want a gift, but I wanted a special date planned out completely by him, knowing in my heart there wasn't anything he could've planned that would make me feel appreciated as a wife. There was nothing he could've done to make me feel special; nevertheless, I wanted him to try. I wanted him to put in the effort to see me.

To my dismay, he took the easy way out and bought me a health activity watch, which I later returned. It's possible the watch was his way of showing me he cared by taking my health into consideration. For him, my health was more important than a date. I interpreted it, in that moment, as a lack of love. I felt he disliked me and couldn't stand the sight of me. For me, the watch was his way of telling me I was fat and unattractive.

However, even if he had planned a date, my perception wouldn't have changed. I still would've felt unloved. It was a no-win situation for him, and he knew it.

But that's what I've done our entire marriage: set him up to fail. Some of my ways were inherited; some were just me. Either way, I ultimately had to come to the realization that it was never him and had always been me. I said I wanted him to attempt to see me, simultaneously knowing that wouldn't be enough, either. I was expecting him to see me when I couldn't see myself. My sense of invisibility had absolutely nothing to do with him and everything to do with me.

-

At the time, I didn't realize I was blaming him for everything; therefore, when he didn't change I reverted back to what I knew. Attention and I would reunite, like long lost lovers. Once again, I'd blush and become flattered when another man told me how beautiful I was. When any man told me my husband was a lucky man, my ego would soar and so would my high. Those words were the pinnacle for me. They knew he was lucky. I definitely knew he was lucky, but he was the blind one!

Why couldn't he give me what I so desperately needed? Why did I have to leave the house to become visible? The only explanation I could conjure was that I was stuck. I was stuck back in my invisible childhood. I was still that invisible girl at church and home, blending in, turning to the outside to be seen. It was clear that having lived as an invisible child, and then as an invisible woman, the road to destruction was well paved.

SEVEN

"Quiet Wife"

I've spent my entire marriage attempting to make everyone's life easy as I blended into the background. I had it all together, had everything figured out, and it worked for everyone, except me. I was so good at fading into the abyss yet running the house smoothly, never voicing my needs, desires, wants, or thirst. Everyone expected me to do what I've always done, to put my priorities on the backburner for theirs. The main problem with that is, leaving something on the burner too long will cause it to simmer away until there is nothing left. The very things I did to be a good wife, deserving of attention, are the things that made me invisible.

My husband didn't see when I was tired, frustrated, irritated, in desperate need of a mommy break. He didn't see my need of some "me" time, or above all, my need of water in the weary land of our marriage. I was thirsty! I am certain we both were, and I was disintegrating into a mere hologram on my way to nothingness. I just couldn't bring myself to say anything.

I am outspoken in public, but I am very reserved and quiet when it comes to being a wife, another behavior I'd learned from my parents' marriage. I process a lot of things in my head, but rarely verbalize them. Although, I'd told my husband I needed more attention and compliments, he didn't know how this lack affected me deep down in my soul or how invisible I felt.

He would try to connect with me in more affectionate ways, but it felt forced and awkward. There've been times when he'd touch me, and it was as if he had to will his hand to rub my back. It was more similar to a pat you'd give your puppy as he walked by. If I were to respond to this forced dog pat, it would have been a sarcastic comment, thanking him for the pat on the back. Instead, I remained quiet and invisible.

Tender caresses had become so foreign to both of us, they were extinct. There were no hugs or kisses between us. We simply had transactions and conversations that focused on our children, our home, our superficial needs, and our bills. My existence was so robotic and empty; anyone could easily step in and take my place as a wife. It wouldn't have been hard as long as she could be a home manager, living life by a checklist.

One of the items on my checklist was sex. Quiet sex. I used my daughter as an excuse for quiet sex. I rationalized it in my mind by saying I didn't want her to hear anything, but in reality, making any sounds would force me to be conscious. I would have to engage in an act, faking it. I would have to consciously remind myself to release an "ooooh" or "ahhh" at just the right moment. Faking it would mean I would have to at least be present.

I once told him how long it had been since I'd had an orgasm, and he couldn't believe I'd kept track. When a woman feels as if she may as well leave her vagina on the bed and walk away, she notices the few times her entire body got to be involved. When sex was quick and he didn't take the time to notice if I enjoyed it or reached a climax, I felt selfishly compelled to take inventory of what was lacking. There was no foreplay, flirting or mood setting to bring me into the moment of hot desire. Quiet sex is the kind of sex that allotted me time to go over my day and strike "sex with husband" off my list.

I had definitely hit a point in my life where sleep was preferred over sex. I wanted him to notice that I was not really there. I needed my ego stroked! Stroking my ego during sex was a language I understood. My 20-year-old self would ask my 40-year-old self, "What the hell are you doing? Since when did you become this desperate little housewife waiting on your husband to show you some attention, affection, and love? Waiting on your husband to act like he enjoys having you as a wife?

Waiting on your husband to look at you as if he really wants you? Waiting on your husband to notice you when he makes love to you? Since when do you fake it?"

Kizmat at 20 would assure me I still had it, that I could get some quality ego-stroking elsewhere! She let me know I didn't have to settle for a life of this. Young Kizmat always let me know I didn't have to play second fiddle to anyone or anything because I had that good stuff. She told me that he should be thanking his Maker to have all I had to offer. However, Young Kizmat was a fool, and I allowed her to convince me I didn't need to be present during sex, that it was his job to make me become present. She convinced me that good sex was inherently connected to how much HE told me HE wanted me or how good it was to him.

Twenty-year-old Kizmat was immature and childish. So I had to learn to tell her to shut up! I shut her down and decided to be present when with my husband, to carry intimacy with me throughout the day and into the bedroom. I was old enough now to know good sex was when two people formed a connection that reached deeper than bodies pressed against one another.

One day while having sex, he kissed me on my neck, and it was the best kiss ever. I, for once, felt he was listening to my body. He had finally begun to take notice of my needs and wants. The kiss said he wanted me, and it made me want him. The kiss kept me present and aware in that moment. I didn't think about how quick it would be over or whether or not I would have an orgasm. I forgot about my to-do list and all of the other things that normally occupied me during sex. I didn't bring idiotic 20-year-old Kizmat with me this day. I became conscious and present — not to fake pleasure, but to engage in the moment, to enhance it. I came with a mind and heart to yield myself fully to him, trusting him to read me on a deeper level. When our bodies connected, it wasn't like before. This was a new experience. It was finally happening! True intimacy.

I had shared my feelings about our intimate experience with my husband, but I had neglected to tell him I wanted the intimacy to extend beyond our bedroom. Fear of rejection and disappointment swallowed me up. I was too afraid to tell him I wanted him to wrap me in his arms as I sat on the couch. Apprehension clasped my mouth before I could tell him I desired a tender forehead kiss when he saw me sitting at my computer. I wanted to feel wanted always and I wanted my body and soul to respond.

Yet I didn't ask for any of those things. I was too afraid he wouldn't listen to my request and would view it only as another chore, another wrong that he couldn't right. Moreover, I didn't want to give him every detail. I wished he would intuitively know these ways to show me love. I wished he knew my unspoken request was my view of love. I remained, the Quiet Wife.

EIGHT

"Astroturf Life, Astroturf Wife"

Had more people looked beyond the superficial, like my friend, they would've known the grass wasn't greener on my side. It was only green because it was AstroTurf; it wasn't even real grass. I was living an AstroTurf life and was an AstroTurf wife.

My continued silence ushered me seamlessly back to life before marriage. My husband had never gotten all of me because I was guarded. The fear that prevented me from sharing my heart with him stemmed from a heartbreak that occurred long before I met him. While I truly yearned for intimacy to grow between my husband and me, the baggage I hadn't unpacked interrupted our flow.

I've only been genuinely hurt in a relationship once. I was

devastated due to the breakup of this relationship because I'd given my heart to him. Prior to him, I dated only men who had the right education, pedigree, and bank account, and I was always finding ways to manipulate them. I hadn't given my heart to anyone before, but he was different. I wanted him solely for him. Money, status, or fame didn't matter. I would've taken him even if he were broke and busted. I thought I loved him because life seemed easy; with him, I felt like I could just be me. We had fun, I enjoyed being around him, and the feelings were requited.

When we ended I couldn't make sense of it. Our relationship was over because of hearsay spread by manipulative people. I was experiencing, firsthand, how it felt to be on the receiving end of manipulation tactics. Someone else pulled the strings, and this pain was hard. This heartbreak gave me a touch more compassion for others. I truly grieved for the men I'd hurt by this kind of vindictiveness.

However, the compassion I gained wasn't enough to usurp the

pain I felt. I put up a reinforced protection system after that. My guard was strong, and I backslid to the old Kizmat. I was, once again, the girl who selfishly dated only for herself. I should have allowed that experience to change me more, but I didn't.

I still had my defenses up, years later, when I married my husband. I know now that love can't be experienced, at it's fullest, with a guard separating the two hearts involved. I'd said I didn't want to spend weekends with my man with a glass between us, but here I was, so many years later, spending life with my man, and there was a glass between us. There was a glass that I'd placed there myself. I was trying to give and receive love through a barrier. This was another problem in my marriage.

He never got my whole heart, just the part that I chose to share with him. I'd gotten married for all of the same reasons I dated: money, status, and pedigree. I wanted intimacy, and had it that night when we were so wrapped up in each other's love and souls, but my guard kept me silent thereafter.

I was back to pretending, and outsiders only saw the surface, never allowed to view the depths within me. They saw the house, the car, the marriage, the kids, the vacations, the date nights, and they thought we were living the good life. They assumed the grass was greener here. "Goals!" That's what someone once said upon entering my house. I silently chuckled because anyone can obtain a mortgage, a car note, debt, you name it.

I wanted to say, "No, Love, don't strive to have my house. Strive to find your true and authentic self. Strive to find love that you can be secure in. Strive for true intimacy and not just sex. Strive for things that can't be seen, but that can be felt deep down in your soul. Strive for a relationship where he not only sees you, but also sees into you. He sees when you're tired. He sees when you need a hug. He sees when you need a touch. He sees when you just want to be held. Seek a spiritual connection. Many don't know there's a difference between a marriage filled with love as the binding agent and a marriage that is empty but has appearance as the binding agent. So, sweetheart, if a house is your only goal, then you don't have many goals at all."

The next time you want to make someone's marriage your goal, don't just listen to what they're saying but also to what they aren't saying. Don't put confidence in what they're doing, but rather gauge what they aren't doing.

I'd just begun writing *Invisible Wife*, and was talking with a friend about it. I told her that my husband was going to be very surprised once he read how I felt about our marriage. She candidly responded, " You know, I have never seen true love and affection in your marriage; even when you two attempt to hug or touch, it's always seemed forced and unnatural. You guys are very cordial to one another, but I've never seen that passion that one would expect to see in a marriage. It's like you two just tolerate one another for the sake of being married." I confessed to her

I'd felt the same way for years and had thought about leaving numerous times.

Had more people looked beyond the superficial, as my friend did, they would've known the grass wasn't greener on my side. It was only green because it was AstroTurf; it wasn't even real grass. I was living an AstroTurf life and was an AstroTurf wife.

NINE

"Illusionist"

I was known for being direct and speaking my mind outside of my home. I always went after what I wanted. It was all about CONTROL.

For those of us who seek to control everything, the root of that desire is fear and hurt. We fear if we aren't in control, it will cause us to be weak and vulnerable. It puts us in a position where others may take advantage of us. As a result, we control in order to avoid being controlled. We control love, relationships, friendships, money, situations, circumstances, you name it. We control our marriages and our kids.

I never realized how thin the line was between control and manipulation. I used to brag about my ability to control people and get anything I wanted. I was boasting to an old friend about my ability to control others, and she said, "You know, according to the Bible, manipulation is a form of witchcraft."

I responded, "Well, I just think I'm very charming and persuasive." Surely, being charming wasn't a sin. I couldn't be a witch just because of my God-given abilities. Surely, not. Wasn't I supposed to be a go-getter? I was only endeavoring to improve my quality of life by maintaining an optimal level of happiness.

She said, "Exactly. That is witchcraft: the fact that you do all of this specifically to get your way or to get something from them."

I contemplated this notion for a moment. Witchcraft? I actually thought manipulation was simply a gift. I was even proud of that gift. This conversation was eye opening for me. I reflected on the amount of work it took for me to come up with all the necessary stratagems to manipulate others and execute those plans successfully.

By definition, sorcery is the use of magic through spells, enchantment, or witchcraft. Wow! All the planning I had to do to control others would fall into these categories. I'd used charm, wit, carefully uttered words, and a myriad of masks to work my sorcery. I used a plethora of masks to transform myself into someone else, and when I morphed into that role, my presence was always acknowledged, and I'd get what I came after.

Every mask I wore was custom fitted for every occasion. With the masks, I could smile while being plagued with sadness and laugh without showing my inner pain. I could pretend all was well with my soul even though hell was breaking loose on the inside. I had a mask for the facade of being a happy wife. Illusions of happiness and freedom were conveyed with every mask. I could hide all of my insecurities, doubts, hurts, disappointments, shame, regret, hopelessness, and tears. I transformed, morphed, and put on a show of illusions with little thought after I'd mastered my craft.

The effort was so minimal, at some point I stopped seeing my true self even when I was alone. I was continually wearing a mask, working my sorcery. Instead of my controlling the magic, it began to control me. It merged itself into me, and I lost track of when I was operating in "my gift" and when I wasn't. It became impossible to keep up with it. I couldn't remember which mask I'd shown to whom. Did I present happy Kizmat, feisty Kizmat, sexy Kizmat, Life Coach Kizmat, or religious Kizmat? One thing is for certain; I had been dabbling in this sorcery for many years unbeknownst to myself. If my friend hadn't cared enough for me to tell me, straightforwardly, that I was operating in the spirit of witchcraft, I may have continued through the rest of my life, thinking I was so powerful because I knew how to manipulate and control people and situations to feel accomplished.

I may not have stopped to ponder why I was so insecure that I'd resorted to manipulation in order to make myself feel better at at the expense of my marriage, my kids, my friends, and family. I'd really done a number on my husband. What I thought to be an asset had been revealed for what it truly was, and I was revealed for what I truly was: an illusionist.

TEN

"The Real Him"

I can't blame my husband for perfecting the mask I'd given him. Men don't read minds; they take direction. I gave him the mask, and then I became angry because he wore it so well. He became everything I wanted and hated at the same time. I created my very own Frankenstein, and I had to suffer the consequences of dealing with a monster that looks just like me. Misery loves company.

Living with a master illusionist couldn't have been easy for my husband. In fact, I know it was extremely difficult for him. I'd, single handedly, managed to force a mask on him. I needed him to be what I thought I wanted.

When I first met my husband he was fun, high energy, and romantic. He had one of the biggest and most beautiful smiles I had ever seen. He had the ability to smile with his eyes, which made him even sexier. He was tall, dark, and handsome, just the way I liked them. He was kind, polite, and he always went above and beyond to show me that he cared. He had such a gentle spirit, and he could have had his pick of many women.

He would attend my son's football practices and games without my having to ask him. He gave me whatever I asked for, regardless of the cost. He even cooked dinner for one of my girlfriends and me. It wasn't just any dinner; he laid out a full three-course meal! He was what any smart woman would want in a man. Unfortunately, I wasn't that type of girl. I liked cool and laid back guys who played just as hard to get as I did. I liked guys who weren't so predictable and available. I liked the guys who kept me guessing and wondering if they were truly faithful.

I was a fun, yet laid back type of girl, and meeting someone like him was foreign to me. It had to be too good to be true. I didn't think I was insecure and doubtful, because I've always felt like I was a good catch. At least that's what I used to tell myself. I had convinced myself that I could have anyone I wanted. Even being a single mom didn't diminish my perception of how pretty I was. I was very confident and too arrogant for my own good.

He would show up when I didn't want him to. At one point I told him that I couldn't do it; I couldn't see us together. I let him in only close enough to hook him, and then I let him go. I was still playing that tired cat-and-mouse game from my childhood church days.

One night, while hanging out with two of my closest friends, we had a "Come to Jesus Meeting" about him. They convinced me he was a nice guy and would be a great husband and a great father to my son. They convinced me he could be trusted, and he would be a great person to spend the rest of my life with.

I later met with someone in the church who offered her opinion as well. She told me I shouldn't judge him based on the car he drove, because she'd seen his financial statements, and he made very good money. She convinced me my son and I would be well taken care of. Between her comments and my friends, I figured maybe he was the right person for me, even though in my heart I felt differently.

Despite my misgivings, I accepted him and imposed conditions on him concerning the way he needed to conduct him around me, and he complied. Instead of trying something new, I turned him into the type of guy that I was used to. I compelled him to calm down. I told him that he was too over the top and I didn't like it.

It was weird to me when he was romantic because that's not what I was accustomed to. I never saw my dad being romantic to my mom, and I honestly never had anyone be romantic towards me. As a result, I thought his idea of romance was corny.

I remember attending an event at church, and when I arrived, he had chosen different people to bring me roses. Would you believe that I was more embarrassed than I was flattered? I felt like he was drawing too much attention to himself and us. Reflecting on it now, he was everything then that I want now.

I couldn't see who he saw because I didn't know myself. Perhaps I was afraid that he would wake up one day and realize that I was a fraud, and see I was just another female wearing a lot of masks. My vision was so distorted that I was unable to see clearly. I couldn't see that he was the husband I prayed for. He was everything I wanted, but nothing I deserved.

He was my big guy who I could count on for support. He was the guy who could hold me. He was the guy who made me feel loved and accepted. He was the romantic guy I'd read about in the romance novels. He was all of that and then some, but I was too broken to realize it. I was too broken to appreciate it. I was too broken to respect it. I was too broken to see he was treating me like the queen I always wanted to be.

I was so accustomed to controlling and manipulating my relationships and didn't realize that years of game playing had broken me. Now, here I was, telling him all of these things that I needed 15 years later. And I'm sure he was confused, because when he had tried to give it to me, I didn't want it. He had changed and become the person I wanted him to be. Then suddenly I was telling him that I didn't like that guy.

"You're too quiet. You work too much. You don't show me enough affection and attention. You don't make me feel special. You don't make me feel loved and appreciated. You don't make me feel wanted. You don't make me feel married. You don't make me feel anything good that I need in my life." How do you convince someone to go back to the very person you didn't like in the beginning? If I were him, I would be scared too. I would think, *This lady is crazy, and I'm damned if I do and damned if I don't. I can't win, so why try?*

I've met some really amazing guys in my lifetime. My idea of amazing was based on level of education and pedigree. If a man had a degree, he got my attention because he had something I didn't. A man's parents who were still happily married translated as an amazing guy to me. I wasn't married to my son's father, and a man coming from a two-parent home was attractive. I was like a moth to a flame when I encountered these "amazing men."

I realize the areas that I idolized in men were the areas where I felt inadequate in my own life. I was ashamed that I had dropped out of college because I was pregnant. I was ashamed because I was a single parent, especially if he didn't have kids. My insecurity would overtake me, and I wouldn't want to be presented to his parents as a potential mate, for fear they wouldn't approve.

So, I told myself these good boys could capture my attention but didn't have the ability to maintain it because they were too sweet or nice. In reality, it was more panic and a defense mechanism that led me to dump them before they could dump me. I convinced myself that I didn't like the guy who was predictable, the guy who actually called when he said he would call, or the one who was there when I needed him.

How could a guy who was focused in life really want to be with me? I really didn't have any goals in life at the time, other than to make sure my son and I always looked good. I honestly felt that there were some guys who I would ruin. So, I intentionally sabotaged the relationship or broke it off because I knew I wasn't good for them. I really didn't understand what they saw in me, because I didn't really see anything in myself.

I gave my husband a mask to wear, and I don't know if he's ever taken it off. Perhaps he removes it in my absence. Others may be privileged enough to see the authentic him.

I remember a time when a family member, on my husband's side, was going through a tough time. It was during a family gathering, and I remember walking outside and seeing my husband holding her. I felt so angry because he'd never held me like that, and being held like that was something I needed. How could he comfort someone else when he'd never taken the time to comfort me?

In fact, if I got into his personal space it seemed to be a turnoff. I felt as if he didn't want me to be close to him. He would often jump when I touched him, as if a stranger just violated his body. Maybe it really was a violation of his body since he didn't know the true me. He married one of my masks, and he probably didn't know which mask he'd see at any given moment.

I am certain people thought or assumed they were getting a glimpse into my marriage. They probably thought I had such a good man, who was emotionally supportive and in tune with my needs. Surely any man who could take the time to wrap his arms tightly around a relative, to affirm she would get through the rough patch, had to show greater concern, love, and empathy towards his wife, right?

I have a very selective memory, and the things I choose to remember are never forgotten. The intimate moment I witnessed between my husband and his family member is a moment that I will never forget. I can't. Erasing this memory is impossible because, in that moment, he unknowingly revealed to me what he was capable of. His actions that day said to me, " With the right woman, I can pour out love and compassion." In that moment, he showed me that maybe I was not the one for him, and maybe he was not the one for me. That was insecurity speaking to me. I now know he was being himself, the real him. He didn't have to wear a mask while being there for his family. She needed comfort and was open to receiving it.

Now I view this day from a different lense. What I witnessed was meant to tell me I did have someone to comfort me, but I needed to be open and available to it. He would give me the real him, if only I'd show some sign that he could remove his mask without repercussion. If he could, allowing me to once again see the man I met, I too could have love, compassion and support.

Maybe he was crying out in that moment, too. Instead of raging on the inside, I wish my eyes could have seen what he was truly showing me in that moment. Had I understood the lesson, as it was being taught, I would have had the courage to remove my mask, too. Instead, I let pride get in the way, and everything continued as it always did. We both wore our masks.

I have pondered the notion that he may have worn the mask to protect himself from me. If that is the case, I couldn't blame him, but I did miss him. I missed the husband and father he would've been. How could he have lived with someone who' had never accepted the true him for so long?

Now you see how wearing a mask and being invisible had shaped my entire life. I'm still dealing and living with the consequences of those masks. We are currently still married, but for years I have wondered why. I was not aware of the damage that I'd done, until I began writing this book. I wasn't aware of the masks that I'd been wearing or that I'd given until I embarked on this journey. This process has my mind wide open.

Although my husband is truly an amazing guy, I feel bad. I regret having created his mask. I hate that he ever accepted it. I wish he hadn't. He never should have allowed me to change him. Allowing me to take his joy and smile never should've been an option. Trusting a woman who couldn't trust herself was a mistake. He should have run and never looked back.

In fact, I think a part of him did run, because I haven't seen that side of him since I gave him that custom mask. I carry the remorse of knowing there are people in our lives who have never known him without the mask. They would've really loved the real him. He would've been the life of the party, every kid's dream dad, and every woman's dream husband. If only I could turn back the hands of time. If I could have been in a position to receive love, I could have remained faithful.

ELEVEN

"True Living"

Unfaithfulness has begun to have various meanings for me. In the past, I would correlate unfaithfulness with sexual infidelity, but now it seems to have taken on a completely different definition in my life. Unfaithfulness is not limited to physical intercourse outside of your marriage, but it can be mental infidelities. I've learned that it's not my actions that I was afraid of but my thoughts. My thoughts revealed my double mindedness. I frequently wondered if I made the right choice or not. I couldn't decide if I could stay in this marriage until death do us part, or not.

Is the true love of my life still out there, or am I already married to him? Can our marriage be reconciled or not? Thoughts of staying or going plagued my mind. Does he share the same feelings and thoughts as I do? All of these thoughts, questions, and feelings had an effect on my trust.

I recently realized every thought I'd projected onto him was my own feelings. The questions concerning his thoughts of marriage were really my own. It's easier to project so that it appears to be the other person's fault. I was too cowardly to acknowledge my own feelings and used him as a scapegoat. It would be much easier if he asked for a divorce, admitted that he wasn't happy, or that he had regrets from the beginning.

It wasn't him; it'd always been me. I'd always had doubts. I'd been unfaithful, not physically, but in my heart, to both of us. I had checked out emotionally from the marriage, searching for an out for years, but I never had the courage to say it.

Now, I was telling myself it was time to fight for my marriage. I was willing to do whatever it took for us to thrive. I wanted and needed to do this the right way this time. This fight was going to be the toughest fight of my life not because I was fighting him but because I was fighting myself. I was fighting my feelings, thoughts, emotions and years of frustration.

Exhaustion and fear had become very real, but I wouldn't allow feelings of defeat to overcome me. I was in a boxing ring, prepared for the battle. This would be the most crucial fight of my life, battling my mind, ego and pride. So I prayed and told God I couldn't do this without Him. I desperately needed Him to take this, and I promised Him I'd show up.

We always pray and say we'll give it to God, but this time, I really needed Him to take it. I was unable to win the battle of my mind without Him.

I originally thought this chapter would be about my husband, but it's really all about me. I had never squared off against myself, but now I had to do it for the sake of my mind and myself. I had to do it for the sake of my marriage and children.

Here I stood, toe-to-toe with myself, fighting for my freedom. When the masks came off, I had a face-off with myself. My natural instinct would be to put the masks back on, but they weren't coming back.

I assumed the mask removal would allow me to breathe easier; instead, my breathing was rapid. I was scared and feeling exposed. I wanted to flee and slam the panic button, but I had to stay in the moment. I had to feel this in order to process what was happening. No more running. No more hiding. No more deflecting. No more dismissiveness. I had done that all of my life, and it was time to stop.

This was my new beginning. I would experience true living. Sweeping issues under the rug, hoping you don't trip over them later, is not true living. Open mindedness, transparency, and owning my emotions, gave way to true living. True living is learning how to have healthy disagreements and not be intimidated by differences. True living is compromise, respect, and communication. True living is when you decide to stop being unfaithful to yourself and those you love. Living authentically begins then.

TWELVE

Create Music?

Our fears only have power when we are unwilling to face them. Fear of the unknown, being alone, or even exposed — take the power away from the fear, and put the power towards your growth. What you have done will never change, but your perception can change immediately. No one will ever judge you more than you have already judged yourself. You are much tougher on yourself than any other human can ever be. Every time that fear or regret bears it's ugly head, remind yourself how much you have grown and how far you have come. Growth is not living a perfect life. Growth is making a mistake and taking the time to learn from it.

Regret and perfectionism are companions. We fear having regrets, thus, propelling our mindset into the ways of perfectionism. Our minds set up a home there, and we succumb to the illusion: Mistakes are not allowed. We must shift our mindset and hearts to comprehend mistakes and give ourselves the opportunity for maturity and knowledge. These two elements give us an opportunity to feel, process, and move on from the pain of poor decisions.

It is certain that some of our mistakes may carry consequences we have to live with for the duration of our lives, but we still can grow from them. Don't allow your regrets to keep you handcuffed and bound. Don't allow the shame from your regrets to be your silent killer. Free yourself and make it a point to help someone else that is about to walk down the same path or already has.

You need to know you're not the only one who's done things you're not proud of. I'm certainly not proud of some of my decisions, but I can't live with the guilt and shame of my regrets, knowing I can't go back and change any of my bad decisions. I hope my story has helped you or will help someone you know. My story has certainly helped me.

This book completely rocked me to my core, but I wouldn't have it any other way. I've been stripped down to the raw meat, ripping off all the masks and becoming visible. This entire book has been centered around facing myself and being afraid I may not like what I saw. You can no longer live in that prison. Maybe you don't have to go as far back as your childhood, as I did. However, for me, it was necessary to gain a better understanding of how feeling invisible as a child played out in my entire life, and to understand the part it played in my marriage. I had to pull back the layers that have been piled on for years.

As you begin peeling the layers, you may find it's easier with the help of a professional. Don't allow the stigma of seeking professional help to keep you from uncovering the true and authentic you. It takes more courage and strength to recognize that you need help, and it is not a sign of weakness.

I allowed feeling invisible to become my norm because it was all I knew. The minute I began exposing my life was the minute I began rediscovering who I am. I believe when it comes to finding yourself; it really boils down to the things that no one knows about you. I am talking about those intimate things that you hold close and dear to your heart. The things about you that others may find corny or a waste of time — those are the heart matters I am speaking about.

I realized recently that I'm a hopeless romantic. I love LOVE. I love it when a man isn't afraid to verbally profess his love for his woman. I think we often are afraid to express our wants and desires for the sake of not appearing needy. Whatever! Call me needy; I'll take it. If needy means I get to feel loved and cherished, then I'll take it. If needy means I get to cuddle and have longs talks with someone I love, then I'll take it. If needy means taking the time to enjoy the things in life that make me feel great, then I'll take it. If all of those things define needy, then I have a lot of catching up to do! Give me the shirt that says needy, and I'll wear it.

Because I don't live romance, I lost myself in romance novels. I

allowed the stories to satisfy needs
and desires I wanted for my own
life. I loved the passion and the fight
for love, because I wanted to feel as
if someone out there would fight for
my love. I wanted to feel as if
someone would risk it all to be with
me, to love me. I loved to imagine
that someone couldn't fathom life
without me. I got wrapped up in
thoughts of what it would be like to
be the apple of someone's eye, and
to be that person's central focus.
What would it be like if someone
lived and breathed Kizmat? I
wanted to know the comfort of an
unquenchable and insatiable love
that would compel someone to still
love me on my dirtiest and darkest
day.

I have begun to show my
husband my real face. He is seeing
me without any masks, and we are
getting to know the real Kizmat
together. I am no longer an invisible
wife, because I am no longer
invisible to myself. I had to see
myself before anyone else could be
able to. My husband is seeing my
intimate parts: the opaque past, all
my wounds and scars. And he still

wants me. No faults or shortcomings can keep him from me. He sees me.

I feel like he's still there, even after he leaves. We have intimacy that flows deeper than sex. We have the intimacy that creates staying power and commitment. Letting go of my masks allowed him to let go of his, and now we have created something beyond what I could have imagined. We have created lovely music together. We are creating the musical score of our lives through love. I can only describe it the way I would describe the music of my favorite violinist.

I feel his music deep in my soul, and in my head. This is what heaven feels like, a place where the sound of the strings pulls on my heart. The pulling of my heart with the sounds of the strings confirms that I'm alive on the inside. I know my heart still pumps the blood of life because it beats in perfect timing with the pace of the strings being played. And it accelerates and slows, with crescendos and decrescendos, of the rhythm and beat. It feels like hope and love.

The sound calms my mind, and it feels as though my blood is rushing through my body awakening every cell. It feels like a body orgasm that slowly massages all of my senses, allowing me to be lost in a sea of ecstasy. I've never been high, but it feels the way I imagine a drug would draw me in and take me to places I've never been. It touches me in places that I have never been touched. It sends shivers down my spine while soothing me all at the same time. I imagine this is what it must feel like to be on the brink of ecstasy and insanity. I can close my eyes and just drift away, lost in the sound and rhythm, but feel visible at the same time.

This is what I am experiencing in my marriage now that I am no longer an Invisible Wife. I'll no longer simply exist within my marriage without truly living and loving him or myself. This is new. This is strange, but I know this is the right path for me. In fact, it's the only path for me.
I am breathing.
I am living.

I am free.
This is what life feels like when you
begin to see.
I am no longer invisible.
I See Me.

The End

Broken Little Pieces
Book 2
The Invisible Baby

The Prologue

I'm tired. I'm really, really, really tired — from being mom, wife, teacher, tutor, taxi, nurse, coach, and all of the other million titles and hats that a mom wears in a 24-hour day. I don't even think I enjoyed wearing all of those hats. I was just doing what I was "supposed" to do as a stay-at- home mom.

We all know that as stay-at-home moms, we're supposed to have this unrealistic list of impossible things that we do in a day to justify and prove to the world that we actually do stuff during the day. And did I mention that it was never my intent to become a stay-at-home mom? I was forced into this role while I was pregnant with my daughter. My son was injured in school and was homebound, needing full-time care for the remainder of the school year. I had to quit my job and basically nurture him back to health. The role never felt natural for me and, to be honest, I'm not sure why I stuck with it for so long. It went against everything I was as a woman: independent and used to having my own money. In the end, it became another mask that I wore. And, of course, I was going to be the overachiever and wear that mask to the best of my ability.

Everyone in our home just went along with my new role. Only years later did I find out that my husband resented the "stay at home" Kizmat as much as I did. He had fallen in love with the corporate Kizmat, which were the words that he once used to describe the woman I used to be. And there I was, secretly hating what I had become, and he was, too.

But I was also a little angry at his words, because I made his life really easy. Yes, he went out and made the money to pay the bills, but his list of responsibilities probably stopped there. And he had the nerve not to be appreciative. But then again maybe he was appreciative. You can be appreciative of what someone does for you in a marriage and still not really care for them as a spouse.

After five years of marriage, we almost called it quits. I think we were both tired of faking it and pretending that this marriage thing could work for us. But, unexpectedly, I became pregnant. How in the world did I end up pregnant while seriously considering divorce? I swear, I felt like the Virgin Mary, because I seriously don't remember us having sex during that time. I was so upset with God for allowing that to happen. God knew that our marriage was screwed up and bringing another child into this world was the last thing we needed!

I don't even know if my husband realized that I spent the entire pregnancy planning life without him. I had figured out where he would live and where I would live with the kids, so that they would still feel connected to him. I had it all planned out and I don't think he had a clue. I was done with this marriage! I was not a stranger to being a single mom, because that's what I was when I met him. I was single and doing quite fine with just me and my son. Adding two more kids to the mix was not going to require me to miss a beat. I was not afraid of that life and knew that I was perfectly capable of handling things on my own. It was like I was carrying this big secret and nobody knew. He was going to be out just as soon as my baby was out. Ironically we came up with the name of Justus for the baby before he was born. Pronounced "Just-Us", this baby was about to be born into the "End of us" as a marriage.

On the day that I went into labor, I knew that my life would never be the same again. If someone had told me the reasons why, I don't think I would have ever believed them. I never would have believed that on September 16, 2008, I would be in labor delivering my son hours after hearing that he didn't have a heartbeat. During labor, I remember thinking that my marriage must have been so screwed up that even God knew that bringing another child into this marriage was a bad idea. But I could have managed. *It didn't have to end this way, God. I could have taken care of my kids on my own.*

This was not in the plan. I hadn't planned on the death of my baby, only my marriage. I was supposed to be planning his crib placement in the room, not a place to bury his ashes. Didn't God know that his big brother and sister were waiting on him to complete our family? His dad would not have been in the home, but he still would have been a great father. I was not prepared for God's plan. I was not in control. I had no words. I had no plan B. I don't even think I had tears at the time.

The first time that I have ever heard my husband cry was after I delivered Justus. As he was crying, he simply kept apologizing for not being there. He felt the disconnect in our marriage as much as I did. Who knows, maybe he had secretly been planning his out as well. So as he was crying, I could only wonder how far he had emotionally strayed from our marriage and my pregnancy to feel so broken in that moment. Maybe he was sad because he never felt the kicks or the connection that I felt while carrying Justus. Maybe he was sad because he felt somewhat responsible. Maybe he blamed himself. Maybe he blamed me. Either way, my son was dead, lying in the baby hospital crib right beside me.

It was hard to stare at my baby, so I would sneak glimpses as if I were afraid he would catch me. He was gone, but I wondered if he were up in heaven watching his father cry. I felt so many emotions in that moment. I felt love and compassion, but then I felt hate, disgust, and regret. I wanted to hold my husband and share his pain. But I also wanted to tell him to get the hell off of me you sorry son of a b****. You deserve every pain you're experiencing right now. I wanted to knee him in his mouth while he was lying on my belly crying. I knew in that moment that my response would determine the outcome of my marriage. I knew that I could go ahead and put the dagger through his chest. I knew that my words in that moment had the power to give life or death to my marriage. I remember just staring at him.

My chest was rising and falling with every deep breath because I knew that something was about to come out of me, but I just didn't know what. He didn't deserve my compassion. He didn't deserve my comfort. He didn't deserve my kids. He didn't deserve me. And just when I thought I couldn't take him even touching me anymore, with one deep long breath, I felt God's grace. I felt God's love. I felt God's forgiveness. And I gave him what I would have wanted God to give me in that moment.

I gave him love. I held him. And as I held him, his cry deepened. I can only assume he had been waiting for my acceptance. He had been waiting for my forgiveness. And in that moment, I felt his pain. He was grieving, too. He lost, too. He lost his first biological son. All of the dreams that he had for Justus died that day as well. All of his hopes died. Everything died on that day.

That morning I sent out a mass text message stating that I was in labor and that Justus was on the way. I later had to send out another mass text message informing everyone that Justus had died. It was probably one of the most defining moments of my life. Yet it was another mask I chose to wear.

I now had the mask of grieving mom. How do I have a perfectly healthy pregnancy with no baby to show for it? What now? What do I do next? How do I recover after my child dies? Where is the manual that tells me what to do next? Who do I call first? How did this happen? Do I still send out the baby shower thank you cards? Would my milk still come in? Did my body even know that he died? How long would I still look pregnant? What about the people who don't know?

God, you clearly have a plan, because this does not make sense. It was not a complicated pregnancy. There were no problems or warning signs. My baby is lying here, looking like a perfectly healthy sleeping baby. He looks like he's sleeping. He looks as if I could just nudge him a little, and he would wake up.

I'm staring at him now, willing him to wake up. Pleading with him to feel my heart and to just wake up. I'm trying to connect with him on such a deep level that only he and I can feel, urging him to wake up. *Wake up for mommy. Baby, I just need you to wake up for me.* God has done it before and He can do it now. *Be the miracle baby. Be the baby that people will testify about. Be the baby that gives people hope. Wake up Justus. Mommy needs you to wake up for me.* But he didn't move. I stared as long as I could and there was never any life in his chest. No baby sounds. No cries. Just more silence. Just like the silence in my home. The Invisible Child who grew up to become an Invisible Wife, now had an Invisible Baby.

To be continued...

Made in the USA
Columbia, SC
15 November 2017